Misprint

JAMES WOMACK was born in Cambridge in 1979. He studied Russian, English and translation in St. Petersburg, Reykjavík and Oxford. He currently lives in Madrid, where he teaches at the Universidad Complutense and is co-editor of the publishing house Nevsky Prospects, which produces Spanish translations of Russian literature. Amongst others, he has translated works by Alexander Pushkin, Vladimir Mayakovsky, Boris Savinkov and Silvina Ocampo. A selection of his poems appeared in *New Poetries V: An Anthology* (Carcanet, 2011).

First collections from Carcanet Press

Caroline Bird, *Looking Through Letterboxes*
Linda Chase, *The Wedding Spy*
Peter Davidson, *The Palace of Oblivion*
Will Eaves, *Sound Houses*
Gerrie Fellows, *Window for a Small Blue Child*
David Herd, *Mandelson! Mandelson! A Memoir*
Julith Jedamus, *The Swerve*
Katharine Kilalea, *One Eye'd Leigh*
Carola Luther, *Walking the Animals*
Kei Miller, *There Is an Anger That Moves*
Gerry McGrath, *A to B*
Patrick McGuinness, *The Canals of Mars*
David Morley, *Scientific Papers*
Togara Muzanenhamo, *Spirit Brides*
Ian Pindar, *Emporium*
Richard Price, *Lucky Day*
John Redmond, *Thumb's Width*
Arto Vaun, *Capillarity*
Matthew Welton, *The Book of Matthew*
Jane Yeh, *Marabou*

JAMES WOMACK

Misprint

CARCANET

Acknowledgements

Thanks to *PN Review* and *The Wolf*, where some of these poems, sometimes in slightly different shapes, have appeared. Poems very like 'Experiment', 'The Dogs of a House in Mourning and the Naked Girl', 'Tourism', 'Vomit', 'Little Red Poem', 'Now, / A / Poem / That is Called / "Of Insomnia"' and sections 5 and 12 of 'Eurydice' were published in *New Poetries V: An Anthology* (Carcanet, 2011). Versions of 'Young Romance', 'The True Scholar', 'Dark and stormys' and sections 6, 7 and 8 of 'Eurydice' appeared in *Voice Recognition: 21 Poets for the 21st Century* (Bloodaxe, 2009).

None of these poems would have been written without the support, forbearance and love of my wife, Marian.

First published in Great Britain in 2012 by
Carcanet Press Limited
Alliance House
Cross Street
Manchester M2 7AQ

A CIP catalogue record for this book is available from the British Library
ISBN 978 1 84777 138 4
The publisher acknowledges financial assistance from Arts Council England

Typeset by XL Publishing Services, Tiverton
Printed and bound in England by SRP Ltd, Exeter

Contents

Eurydice

From a Notebook

What can we do to this word?
Only when you start to write
The poem like a landscape under
    fog   The grain of the paper
Why not possible to make a poem
    like a study for a painting?
Some brilliant areas of detail and
    the rest nothing, plastered, scrubbed out,
full of details that will not
    exist without the reader to make
them. A poem that is only
    a farrago of hints.
Who owns the copyright to an erratum
    slip? Nuance   Stubbs and his horses

The Thing

My favourite B-movie, one of those designed
    to pass the time, rather than say anything,
is a sci-fi romp set in Tudor England
    ('Look, sire! The monasteries... They're... dissolving!')
where Lionel or John or Drew Barrymore
    in padded jacket and transparently false beard
strides up and down the same grey corridor
    that would be stone if it wasn't cardboard

and Douglas Fairbanks Jr. or Sr.
    has a swordfight with Walter Brennan
and Margaret O'Brien or Maureen O'Hara
    has this great moment – it's my favourite scene –
    when she sees The Thing and stops, leans
    back, puts her hands to her cheeks, and screams.

The Water Cycle: Variations on a Theme

I want... I want everything I've ever seen in the movies!
                        Leo Bloom, *The Producers* (1968)

I
Trevi Fountain

In 19 BC, Agrippa built
the aqueduct that would eventually
bring water here. He guessed the iconic image
of Anita Ekberg bathing, he dreamed
of her matronly breasts, he fucked her in his dreams,
Agrippa did – the bastard. Others come and throw a coin
as a charm to return here, thinking unconsciously:
'Maybe the next time she'll be here.'
And they don't see that she is here, bathing,
that her breasts mother the dreams of the eternal city.

after the Spanish of Martín López-Vega

II
Los Angeles Storm Drains

In 1930 AD, the Army Corps of Engineers built
the drainage system which takes
run-off water here. They guessed the iconic image
of Lee Marvin hunting, they dreamed
of his riveted face, they arm-wrestled him in their dreams,
the A.C.E. did – the bastards. Others come and take a photo
as a charm to protect themselves, thinking unconsciously:
'Maybe the next time he'll be here.'
And they don't see that he is here, hunting,
that his face patrols the dreams of the city of dreams.

III
Bethesda Fountain

In 1837 AD, John B. Jervis built
the aqueduct that would eventually
bring water here. He guessed the iconic image
of Zero Mostel capering, he dreamed
of his balloon gut, he bought 50% of 'Springtime for Hitler' in
his dreams,
John B. Jervis did – the bastard. Others come and throw a coin
as a charm for financial security, thinking unconsciously:
'Maybe the next time he'll be here.'
And they don't see that he is here, capering,
that his gut scams the dreams of the Big Apple.

IV
Channel Tunnel

In 1988 AD, Elizabeth II and François Mitterrand built
the tunnel that would eventually
keep the water away. They guessed the iconic image
of Tom Cruise on a runaway helicopter, they dreamed
of his six-pack, they hid their faces behind latex masks in their
dreams,
Mitterrand and Liz did – the bastards. Others sit in a boring train
as a charm for European unity, thinking unconsciously:
'Maybe the next time he'll be here.'
And they don't see that he is here, posing,
that his six-pack hides the dreams of the Entente Cordiale.

V
The Atlantic Ocean

In 130,000,000 BC, the Atlantic Ocean built
the shores that would eventually
divide the waters from the waters. It guessed the iconic image
of Jaws in semi-temperate currents, it dreamed
of the shark's teeth, it saw the fin carving the water in its dreams,
the Atlantic Ocean did – the bastard. Others sunbathe
as a charm for saving an arm or a leg, thinking unconsciously:
'Maybe the next time it'll be here.'
And they don't see that it is here, biting,
that its teeth cut the dreams of Amity, New England.

Halfway through the A-Feature

I liked walking in in the middle of the programme;
you could imagine what happened before.

M.E. Hodges

... the savage ruts in the university grounds,
his costume abandoned to the sodden leaves;
lino loincloth, patchwork posing pouch
all shed as he stalks his latest conquest:
stray cats and virgins, magpies, a Nin's vicuña –
at the indiscriminate moment of orgasm
his head is tilted back and his throat is open, then
credits, five minutes of darkness and ice cream,
and the whole sorry story begins again –
trailers: *The Discreet Charm of the Bourgeoisie 2*:
in a world before time, in a time before space,
a dwarf, a princess, and a renegade monk...
a script that writes itself, tune out till the newsreel –
royal visits, then a brief interview with a Nobel winner
condemned to death for laughter of several kinds
and now locked into a defiant house, smiling,
stroking his cats, whose names – Kaspar Hauser,
Mister Chan – are changed to protect the innocent,
and an artist who has made a collage of Stalin
out of advertising material: his moustache
a McDonald's® M, his fingers Raid® cockroaches –
then the cartoon is *The Last Days of Popeye*:
flight-grounding volcanoes and spinach,
and it all comes out right in the end, then
we feel the theatre shake as the organ sounds
the scary bass notes for the B-movie credits:
an hour and a half with one or two memorable scenes
but hardly *With It's Blood To Shock You Again!*
as the poster had promised; but when the diners
turn into Schütte goblins at a table stained
with acidulated gravy, duck-blood and wine
we jumped a little, and the opening scene's great
with the German exchange, Jessie, at the Ouija board

conjuring a dark *something* that will come back
to haunt them... OK, one and a half thumbs up,
but the main feature is a complete flop:
you know, kind of *arty*... it begins with a shot
of a tramp's mangled hand with nails like claws
on whatever fingers he has left, then turns into
an interminable musing on university types,
the creative writing professor wondering for days
(whole minutes of screen time) if he should skip
from responsibility straight to his pornographic
late phase, horny as Yeats, bed-staining versifier,
and finally (we came in here, hereabouts,
time to get our coats together because we're off),
with the students below like baby figures
in an architectural model, the grey-faced bursar,
a minor character, his kidneys full of grit,
looks down on his domain and notes,
a little annoyed after the cars and the heavy rain,
the savage ruts in the university grounds...

Internet Poems

1 www.defenselink.mil

Caught between
two hyperlinks, the gate of irony
and the gate of porn,
I chose… poorly,

found myself in a scene
of insufficiently lubricated carnage,
live feed from a desert cabin
where a *gosu* the same age

as the internet
worked on his RSI
transforming targets
into slippery sand and jelly

via an Xbox console
and a bank of unmanned
drones on patrol
over a foreign land.

I clicked away ASAP
but the images stayed:
they left me dirty
and untried, played.

2 www.macintoshos.com

I maxed out my credit card
on a gizmo the size of a credit card

which contains all of Mozart
(*Busting Out Of The Bordello*; *Chicks Are Like That*)

as well as audiobooks (Dickens end-to-end
from *Drood, Where's My Car?* to *Our Mutual Fund*)

read, unabridged, by Charles Manson.
Human technology, always advancing.

Young Romance

Look into her eyes and read the answer to the question...
CAN ANY MAN BE TRUSTED?

Let us leave for a moment the bukkake-faced virgin, Our Lady of the pulp magazine, and look instead into her sunglasses.

Although we are – are we? we are – in front of her, the lenses do not reflect us, are no reflection of us, but show instead the same image twice, two people, neither of them us, in a teenage embrace.

But maybe one of them is us, we are either the swooning twin girls or else the pair of rugged heartbreakers, our hairy forearms and manly hands possessing the shoulders of our new beloveds.

We shift position slightly between the lenses, our hands grip the person we love more closely to our differently ruffled shirts.

Three scars prod across our faces, or two scars: the light comes at different angles across our bright background.

We are green, we are green and captured inside our separate black eggs, and then inside their off-white and presumably plastic frames.

And these in their turn are where the watcher's eyes should be: we have replaced her eyes with our kisses and similarly clenched hands.

Her Monroe lips are parted and she has no front teeth, just a brilliant gumshield, and at the ends of her fingers two more little red eggs that reflect the light.

What do we stand before; what is behind us?

What causes these lines of black and whitewash to fall down the unreliable smooth face of her face?

What is coming from behind us?

18

Our background is also cut off, her purple scarf and henna bob filing the boundaries to our vision; even one of our eggs is divided, we can only imagine that it is whole beyond our limits, and that these curtailed but double satisfactions are a true picture, a true reflection of what we are.

Who knows if we can be trusted; who knows?

To the best of our knowledge we have told you what we see, and if these heroes and heroines are not us, then we have no place here.

Three Epigrams

I

The heart forgets its age,
and sees the children
As if it were among them,
and pities the old men.

II

What pleasure there is
in the most formal dances –
Choreography
devised for any agony.

III

The sun against the sea, the sea against the stone –
All against one and all against one.

The Underworld

I

'Some summer we took over, things changed for a season –
hip hop records sampling Tennyson:
Break, break, break... Lives were radios
tuned to the worship of Dionysus,
that god who popped fully-formed from a champagne bottle.
August hotter than July – the streets full of wolves,
and then I was King of the Brooklyn Bridge.

        White pepper blown in the eyes
        is the cure for a scorpion sting
        also the laying-on of hands
        and a swift knee to the groin.
We were given their gods as part of the settlement.
The rebels surrendered, and we left them
to their mistresses and their needles.
But we were given the gods.
    A tip-off took me to his duplex –
Aristaeus, the netter, the trapper, the semi-retired.
Nothing left such a god but to grow old,
to live on his pension as long as he could.
    The whole house stank,
the rancid smell of dips and dicks.
Offertory bowls at his door,
poisoned milk left out for the roaches.
    And the stairs bent under our weight.
A steady bee-hum and drip from the air con.
Thumb-length roaches bobbing in the milk.
    His son hunting spics, his daughter in a back room.
That once-shrewd face, those cunning hands –
a tiny ineffectual god, a god gone mouldy.

We talked to him for a while, but he taught us nothing
and now I remember little of what he said.
In accordance with tradition, he offered us his daughter
and was I thought surprised at our acceptance.'

'Later that evening, at a girl-on-girl in the Aqua Club,
I thought of the daughter, Macris, still locked in my suite.
But the night was still young, and we'd taken her shoestrings.
I appeared to the dancers in a shower of dead presidents.

When I went upstairs later she surprised me –
removing her vest and swaying towards me in the half-dark.
Diana moon in the sky, the sun replaced by street lamps.
I did not see, but to pimp his daughter was itself a wolf trap.
Too soon, quivering inside her, on the edge of orgasm –
                    I had time for one thought
                    Nobody move, nobody get hurt
            before a fatal leap over the edge
            The prairie, a flat river-delta, the tallest towers burning…
            Winter to spring to winter and back again
            the seasons burst and withered in one hotel room.

And I heard Aristaeus crying in the distance
and Macris crying too, both calling their fathers.
The whole town in the grip of its prayers –
Sacrilege, sacrilege, he has wounded the untouchable!

But for one more night, I was King of the Brooklyn Bridge.
One more night, and the sun through the curtains woke me.

I looked out to the day the sun had already tarnished.
Some teens goofing on the street corners.
A too-excited child, his helium balloon
like a hanged man dangling upside down.
The sun moved swearing across my face
so even behind dark glasses my eyes wrinkled.

        And He was there, the binder bubbling where he walked.
        Phoibos Apollo, the far-smiter, god of the wolf-hunt,
        turning the corner of Degraw and Hoyt.
        Incurious, taller than the brownstones,
        summoned as a father and a grandfather
        to see me and raise an annihilating hand.'

III

It was a dark evening, and darkening softly,
and there was something wolfish still
in his eyes and his mouth
as he finished the story and looked up at me.
He wiped his foggy hand on his jeans and held it out
so I could shake it again and remember our deal.

'Let me drink now from your open wrist.
The shades are thirsty, wanderer,
and to talk makes me thirstier still,
and I have told you much, of permanent interest.'

Ariadne

The lights were gone
so I found my way upstairs
by the thin white line
on your red, now black, dress.

Tourism

As the soldiers grow older, they turn native
and grow their beards, against all posted orders.
Duty troops roll in for the tour: they are all naïve,
so keen to pick up the language. Yesterday's doctors

are trading in the city as shoeshine boys,
yesterday's bankers work in second-hand shops –
they deal in tyres and scrap iron and flotsam and toys
made from flotsam and tyres and iron scrap.

Inquisitive cults grow up around petrol
bottles and rags. Religion is being reborn.
The factories work at half their potential.
Psst! Want to know something? Well, not everyone

*has – or wants – a historical homeland they'd love
to return to.* The restaurants are forever
closed for health reasons; the mosques are moved
with the quince trees still inside and the pillars

intact. *Do you want to pay me?* A cold war
leaves ruins, like any other war. Life moves,
only just. Look, dressed in national costume, here
come the women, strapped to their bundles of gifts.

Little Red Poem

If they ask for me tell them I have gone away
to lead my people and be led by them;
to take the thorny path that leads to the light
to struggle, suffer and finally prevail.

Tell them the only home a man can hope for
if he wish to prove his life worthwhile
is the struggle to create a home for all mankind,
not the lone sad fight from one day to the next.

Tell them that if they want me they shall find
my thoughts in others' books, in others' words,
that I am nothing but an honest vessel,
a witness to the truth and not the truth itself.

But do not tell them I am in the attic
behind the false partition, biting my arm in fear,
my gun by my side; that, although reluctant,
I could, at a pinch, employ it for the cause.

freely adapted from the Slovenian

Fish

— So catfish are called catfish because of the whiskers?
— Yes.

Practising Scarlatti:
repeated chromatics, clusters,
the tiny variation
that changes the whole shape
from time to time
the door nudged open
for the cat — rheumy eyes
and a drunk's red nose —
to hear the music
and walk away.

You couldn't just pick it up:
it squirmed and fought
against your fingers
until they knew what it demanded.

One hand at the keys
has its perfect scar
like a bend in the river,
but luckier than that emissary
who lost his right foot
to the goonch in our pool.

Writing *chosongul*
in a blue exercise book,
outside, by the farm's
cascades and rivulets.
What would it be like,
to be a carp, and have the world
expand every time it rained?

One tiny variation
and its rippled outcome.
A week before we left,

drunk deserters from the revolution
sank grenades into the ponds.
A furious remembrance
of those white floating bellies,
the brocaded scales
I always saw as armour.

The Dogs of a House in Mourning and the Naked Girl

The nameless village is burned out
alongside a red clay road dried white.
This is no temporary silence –
April is hot, and the grass stinks.

I came here through a rabbit hole
in the sagged wire fence.
Two dogs ran from a dead house.
I held my camera between us, snapping.

As a child I had a nightmare of wolves
but now I thought of the proverb
Thin as a dog in the house of mourning.
One grey dog, one spotted like a tiger.

Beyond their teeth and noise
was the shadow of something not a dog.
Children in the doorway of a broken building:
a five-year-old girl, a boy, an older girl.

Silhouettes in rags, almost naked;
and in the house two more girls moving faintly.
I couldn't make out their poses or expressions,
I kept taking photographs.

The barking dogs had disappeared.
I went down to the road
and stopped people to ask about it all:
some soldiers, a bus driver, a couple of farmers.

'There are great difficulties involved,
great involved difficulties,
in the proper transliteration of Chinese,'
began Mr Kung (Kong) of
the Art History Department,
as he swatted away some of the bees
that droned like aeroplanes
around the slide projector
in the darkened lecture theatre.
    But by then my mind had begun to wonder
and I caught very little of what followed
[besides, it was *not my field*:
I was a researcher
looking at pseudonyms
in the films
of Maurice Scherer],
but there was something
about the *maîtresse de Matisse*,
and something else, perfunctory,
about the Matrix, *The Matrix*,
but then I nodded off
and came to in a drenched trench,
cut out of time,
where a starving group of guerrillas
were forced to eat grass to survive.
As they nodded to me,
and I felt the rain
through the bright green canopy,
I became somehow unplugged.
I closed my eyes and I was awake again.

Found Poem: President's Reminiscences Read Widely

Working people and school youth and children of the DPRK
are reading with avidity
the reminiscences of President Kim Il-sung
with the approach of the significant Day of the Sun.

Ardent yearning and reverence for the President are read on the faces
of those reading the reminiscences
in the streets, villages, parks and all other places
where spring has come to stay.

The reminiscences of the President *With the Century*
are the most favourite books
of the working people and the school youth and children
among so many books in the country.

They gain extensive and profound knowledge of the revolutionary
history
of the President through the study of the reminiscences,
the library of his revolutionary history
vividly describing it with immensely rich content and gem-like
sentences.

The reminiscences are written in humble words,
but the readers feel with a surge of warmth in their hearts
the immortal feats
of the President in regaining the lost country.

The books give an impressive and historic description
of materials on the revolutionary activities of the President
and stories of actual characters and events.
They also expound the principle of revolution

and depict the struggle and life,
thus leaving deep impressions on the minds of the readers.

The readers learn the theory of revolution,
the principle and ways of revolution

and the noble spirit of loving the country, the nation,
the people and revolutionary comrades

through the reminiscences, the immortal encyclopaedia of revolution
containing the great revolutionary feats
of the President and his noble traits
as a great man.

The reminiscences that appeal more strongly to the hearts and
                                          minds of the people
as the days go by with great influence and persuasive power
are the eternal treasure
of the Korean revolution, a monumental

work which will always hold a special place in human history
and a priceless textbook of revolution.

Property

There they are, these gaps in a non-existent wall,
the twin gateposts, all the standing remains
of boundaries to a number
                              of now-abandoned granges
haphazard across the Cádiz salt plains.
Property is most important – the shells of buildings,
topless towers, walls that are lines in the sand.

Maisky Poems

That man in the courtyard, stretching his fingers,
allowed to stand upright for the first time in years,
is a writer, paid his highest fee yet — his life
for just a few words: his brother, his father, his wife...

I   Anno 1933

The first year in London:
umbrellas and bowler hats;
delicate negotiation
for *placement* and portraits.

It makes a glib adage:
without enough care
any good vintage
may darken to vinegar.

II   To Agniya

Every love story
has an equal and opposite reaction:
to be here is to pay
for the night our best man
like a drunken Gabriel
grabbed you by the lapels:
'You're going to have a daughter,
you're going to have a daughter!'

III   In Scandinavia

A summary of my thousand tasks:
the work of an ambassador
is to eliminate error.
We rode to the north on frozen tracks

then sat by a cold lake
and improved the world:
new order replacing the old
mistake by mistake by mistake.

IV   Three Months in Butyrka

I have become alert to sunshine
to the voices beyond the walls.

A woman calls her children
and I hold my breath until

I hear them, outside with her,
laugh quietly and answer.

V   Spring

Six bent months, and we raise our heads.
The pallid sun on the back of my hand.
And what are these fresh weeds
that stalk the exercise ground?

VI   To My Cell

You are the opposite of home:
your doors close the wrong way.
But you do your job well, and for that deserve
some kind of mechanical thanks.

VII   Prison Sunshine

This irony – light and warmth
enclosed in walls – is not lost on me,
but we cannot avoid happiness
even if we are not happy.

Nature in her summer dress,
birds with their summer loves:
the warders loosen their uniforms,
pull off their rubber gloves.

VIII   Prison Routine

To hold on twenty-two hours at a time
for that bold half-hour each day
when we walk where all the guards observe
and speak via nods, half-glances, winks.

IX   A Year in Butyrka

I am becoming blind to the light,
deaf to the shouts.

In the cell next door a man
calls quietly for his children

and after a terrible hour
one of them, quieter still, answers.

X   To My Judges

I have spent my life
in this way –
been judged for it.
What can I say?

No higher court
exists that can
absolve, forgive
or else explain.

Vomit

Never as sick as after: homemade thick
chicken liver pâté,
½ a bottle of *Stalinswein* (which we bought as a joke,
but no, not funny, not funny…)

The effort I'd been to, the livers so light –
snipping out over the sink
the involved white root –
and the water draining pink.

Then, the lineaments of what I had done, there
on the bedroom floor,
and the room heaved and heavy.
O yes, this was God's plenty.

But as the morning reeled by
all I could remember was the uncooked offal:
these little organs, light as some baby,
and I felt more awful.

Likeness

All northern Russian towns are quite alike
Katia Kapovich

But alikeness isn't that easy, Kat'ka:
alike if you live in them, and walk the Khrushchev courtyards...
Venice is never just a typewritten ST. MARK'S,
or maps of canals and alleys and hidden squares.

It is this warm street and this bright stone:
a place exists in the seeing of it.
And even if I can map Kandalaksha onto Shaitan,
Onega onto Samoded,

who are you to talk of monotony?
So, I might get lost: parks and a bathhouse,
a statue picked from a limited choice
of heroic subjects. Not, no, a world planned for variety,

but I was here, here in these streets and no others.
Vologda, where I unwisely ordered bull's testicles
and showing off fell through a frozen river,
also unwisely; Archangelsk

where we borrowed our bed from a colonel's widow,
ate five-day-old noodles
and saw the whole world
sunken to only the white of a sealed window.

Murmansk, tankers jostling in the Tuloma,
and I had sex above the Arctic Circle
(who else can say that apart from some Eskimos?)
with a woman who was not my wife at all.

They looked the same, but even a tourist's attention
was more than enough, Kat', to distinguish between them.

Experiment

Lived life backwards for a week or so – Ovaltine for breakfast, a long hot bath, bacon and eggs and a pint of coffee at about midnight.

Ten days in, unmoving, nocturnal, costive, bawling for my mother, wearing school uniform again.

Foiled again...

Foiled again, we count our failings.
It starts to rain iron filings.
Dilemmas are hardly ever calming.
The vineyards climb the broken railings.
We huddle to the cliff like lemmings.
The raindrops fall, and keep on falling.

Criticism

I read the same novel as I thought you'd read
but I didn't notice all the characters were dead.

The True Scholar

When they come to write the novel of those years,
you will of course be a minor character,
not having fucked your students,
been an amusing drunk,
or ridiculously addicted to Derrida.

So when M.S., in his soutane
and suntan, has discovered Rome
or the T.M. affair is no more
than a blistering memory
you will be where you have always been:

the coping stone, happy as Pangur's monk
'Bringing difficulty to clearness'.
You will point out, scrupulously,
that this can be read both ways.

from The Literary Encyclopaedia

... but the top position in the annals of solipsism must undoubtedly be ceded to François deBondt (1923-1975), a Belgian who wrote his novels under the pseudo-Japanese pseudonym of Ichi Ije. His first, self-published effort, *Mon Travail* (1948), works under the peculiar constraint of having every event narrated in the first person. Thus, in the opening section, we meet Jean Bonhoeffer, an Alsatian civil servant, hurrying to work:

> I was running down the corridor, afraid of being late. I saw my
> boss.
> I looked him up and down. Bonhoeffer, what a specimen, I
> thought.
> I cringed as I passed him.
> I looked away from the maggot, out of the window.
> In the sky, I was shining brightly.

Ije tried to avoid the foreseeable confusion his technique would cause by providing each of his protagonists (in this instance Bonhoeffer, his superior and the sun) with a distinct typeface. As *Mon Travail* is a novel of some three hundred pages, with a large cast and copious descriptions of the weather, it may be guessed that the variety of printing materials available to Ije in post-Occupation Paris proved scarcely adequate to his ambitions. The publishing house which brought out *Mon Travail* was driven bankrupt, and the type of the novel was broken up.

Perhaps in an effort to minimise costs, Ije's second novel, *Mes Amours* (1959), made fewer concessions to his readers. A pornographic work, every personal or possessive pronoun is replaced by its first person equivalent. In the opening section, we meet Jean Bonhoeffer, a highly sexed Alsatian civil servant, who begins an affair with an attractive young woman in the back room at a cocktail party:

> And I began fumbling with my fly-buttons and I was hoisting my
> dress up and pulling down my panties. I felt my cock with my
> hand and I brought me towards me. I reached my arms up to feel
> my breasts and I felt my tongue in my mouth. I drove forward

with my cock into my cunt and gasped loudly. I felt me put my hand over my mouth to stop me shouting out, or I would have heard myself in the other room, which would have been fatal.

Mes Amours was initially well-received. However, sales drooped before it could reach a second edition. Alphonse Burradeaux, the Belgian literary critic and erotophile, is reported to have said that 'the book is unreadable, for all the wrong reasons'. The publishing house which brought out *Mes Amours* was driven bankrupt, and the type of the novel was broken up.

Ije's final work, *J'arbre* (1975), took fifteen years to find a publisher. It is shorter than his previous novels, only thirty pages in length, but makes up for its exiguousness by its impenetrability. Every single statement in the story is presented as a verb in the first person singular, even the characters' names. In the opening section, we are introduced to Jean Bonhoeffer, an Alsatian, as he takes a walk in the park:

> I tree. I grass. I pond. I ducks. I path. I sunshine. I introduce myself. I Bonhoeffer. I Alsatian. I sun. I shine. I sit. I park bench. I walk. I pretty woman. I follow. I bark. I path. I chase. I catch. I run. I dusk.

J'arbre met with no success at all, was barely read, and sank into obscurity. The publishing house which brought out *J'arbre* managed easily to write off its losses, and eventually pulped the unsold copies. His failure in life drove Ije into a deep depression. His death, aged 52, was a suicide...

Dark and stormys

a

What else should I do
but commemorate
meals and conversations?
It was a night
we drank dark and stormys
rum and lime and ginger ale
and Arima told me
about the end of the world
– an account so detailed
it must be true –
I've not seen her for years
she still writes
or wants to write

b

And a year elsewhere
talking out again
in Reykjavík
– a bent-iron dormitory –
I made dark and stormys
as an inadequate
birthday present
ten of us in the kitchen
juicing limes
rum and ginger ale

Juan Bautista ran in
and called above our gabble
the lights! the aurora!
– all of us on the balcony
in the stairwell –
and the sky split open
a crack above our heads

with the green light dancing
nobody said a word
the light spread above us
to halve the world
This Arima said
this is how it starts

Mosaic

They took off their shoes when they came indoors.

A crooked walking stick propped in the hallstand.

The faucet set in the middle of the kitchen flags.

The saucepan and its boiling egg, a pillar of steam.

But you're my bloody husband! You're my bloody husband!

Indoors, crouched against the unseasonable hailstorm.

Warm milk with honey for her throat, the blue china mug.

How may we fit these fragments together?

All tricks fail. I have tried lying
on my back, my side, on my belly, diagonal;
I have tried less duvet, many
blankets, scooched to the coolest parts of this nocturnal
world, overwarmed them with my flesh.
I am jealous of my sleeping wife and my two cats
dormant nose to anus like a
perverse ginger yin-yang. I have counted quadrupeds,
bipeds, unicycles, counted
the first hundred terms of the Fibonacci series,
counted the clock marking an hour,
and am counting inevitably my ex-girlfriends,
dividing them into two camps:
Inaccessible (Distant), Inaccessible (Dead);
and more sex than I could stand for
nowadays has been recalled, salvaged and catalogued.
I have hoped for inspiration;
have only had memory, physical discomfort.
I am empty. The bedroom is
a black box. I am glad not to remember it all,
to have to remember it all,
save image after image after after-image
on what must be the limited
disc space of my brain. I remember other bedrooms
and car headlights on the ceiling.
My wakefulness has sifted that picture from the night.

Misprint

We'll make him laugh himself o death

Eurydice

i.m. Carlota Castro (1981–2004)

Truly we should guard against conjuring forth the dead in a poetic way in order to call them to remembrance: the most fearful thing is that the dead betray nothing at all.

1

Was it that long ago you died?
It must have been, I suppose.
I remember us in bed:
I couldn't hide my surprise.

Daylight on your wall.
When we are done, there is
nothing to do for a while:
the roof of my mouth buzzes.

The wind and the open window
a bowl of coloured water
your fingers at the piano
the rain's indecent chatter.

But only these remains...
I try to hold your face
complete inside my mind
piece by fading piece.

These months, my memories
wrap themselves together
a clinging knot of images
that time must undo, or sever.

Pray for us sinners, that we have climbed
for ascent's sake only, direction without any goal:
no idea what lies on the hill,
lies round this corner, past this shrine
(*Pray for us sinners*), up these Beauty and Beast stairs…
no one has been here for years.
St Francis's Convent and Ethiopic Museum
and a sign on the wall that I want to translate
as *Please don't feed the penitents.*
The chapel as empty as it can be;
birds preach to each other in the trees.
There is no one here, and I do not know why I fall
to other thoughts – adolescent love in foreign countries.

Adolescent love in foreign countries!
The happy opposite to more serious stuff,
to fortepianism in adulterous affairs:
it is pure crescendo, its end pure melancholy.
Days spent in bed to build a vocabulary,
gestures and suggestions, half-thoughts, faith
that it's only abroad that makes all strange.
Siestas or the white nights turn old sensations new:
Yes, we are the first to have felt like this, so deeply.
The unimprovable true-false alliance
of tourism and affection.

The door closes loudly, we go to the foot of the stairs,
talk about nothing, we don't really talk.
But next to the shrine – *Pray for us sinners* –
you hocus-pocus some words about Catholics,
their pride in the show of devotion.
The sky strains, the air is sweaty with rain.
I point to the flat grass by the Virgin's statue,
the rubbish here and there, the empty bottle of champagne,
and two used condoms, their baby-blue wrappers
tossed onto the downwards path.

The shutters falling, and everywhere the riff of fans. Insupportable heat. Your back like a polished trunk of wood, your arms have the symmetry of branches. Hair in Blossfeldt tendrils. Arching your **IS IT UNGALLANT TO START COMPOSING** back, pushing backwards. If I **THE POEM** could just manoeuvre you so that the **IN THE MIDDLE OF ALL THIS?** striped light through the blinds mapped perfectly to the ribs under your skin. Flesh in my hands. And later, ice water and frozen cherries. No bottle of wine, but the slow juice and almost painful ice. A listless wind stroking the sheets against the tiles.

After, it is you who lie in the hollow of my elbow
   with your legs crooked through mine:
     it is as it looks, slightly uncomfortable.
We are people who have fallen down;
       survivors of some apocalypse or other
couched in our private survivors' glow.
    To be naked in such circumstances is normal
     and we are almost normal, but for
the odd stray sock. It is best to hold on
   for the moment, to feel the waves receding
    and our breathing slow. How many more
    shipwrecks can we expect, how much disaster
will there be time to enjoy? I look again
   into your face, all hopes of rescue fading.

Slowly and patiently we have forgotten it all.
When we made the nails tremble in the headboard
and you rose up with a whisper, the gentle surf moaning.
Underneath the voices, a guitar sounded on the radio.
We believed (at least I believed) in the strength of our arms,
in the precise detail, proof against anything, of our faltering liquid
memories,
in the absolute power of those poems I wrote
when you slid barefoot from bed – I scribbled them blindly,
while you were sleeping,
on any old paper, in a book.
There are so many beautiful, serious, urgent words that will stay
forgotten.
I thought the only worthwhile writing was direct and shameless.

To love you,
while things were like this, while they stayed like this as you slept,
naked,
and I had a scrap of paper, or the wall,
or some blank corner of the planet;
we thought then that the guitar, that damn guitar, would keep on
playing.

Tonight I realise how little life costs, and you and I did not know this.
Tonight a shadow, any shadow
is enough to blow out that strong, eternal, indestructible flame,
any south wind will be enough to blot out my voice.
Memory is water which runs dry
and we cannot (at least, I cannot)
remember for example that other night
which we thought inhabited only by you and me and our words.
(Was it raining? Were we broke? What did we say?)
A man who turns to face the past is blind
because he forgets things twice;
how touching, to try to look with love on the ashes of a love;
as touching as those clowns who contort their bodies by night,
in the middle of the deserted marquee,
and throw their harsh voices into the empty tiers.

after the Spanish of Luis Rogelio Nogueras

6

I

You never told me how boring it is to be mad
with you it was always gin and parties
and the solar radio, that remembered
                  its songs with the sunrise.

II

You were the bright shaman of St. Petersburg
who knew that visions only come
through exhaustion, after the dancing
when you have changed your mind.

III

(And even enlightenment is precarious –
people can fall down stairs and break
the tiny mirrors in their eyes.)

IV

Moments of collapse,
when those enormous emotions
absconded – you couldn't walk
and held my knees on the kitchen floor.
No longer alone, you felt tired –
es ist richtig so, Anna, aber so schwer.

V

Sure we were there
Eden unlost for a month or so
but no more than that, no more.

VI

And we promised to write, but knew we would not.

VII

Outside this window is an empty lawn
the wind embroiders
in silver-green liberty patterns.
   I wake with the fear that I have been
with one who is already dead –
and shuffle to the table
to gather my scattered drafts.

Leaving the bright town to the desert
of three p.m. on a Sunday afternoon.
The immigrants sweeping down the hotel floors.
Half-full buckets, unlicensed cactus pear
on a dusty street corner, the heat of the day
and the lower slopes, past acres of hangdog sunflowers.

Snails cobbling the aloes.
Enough trees to see no more than trees
until you are at them, and they open.
You mount always, over the valley:
a mudslip has slid a *V* from the other hillside.
A moth closes sticky and tight to a sycamore seed.

Not trackless, there are too many paths
through the shade, dead footsteps on the needles
the air claggy, a thin river runs past
without stopping. Climb higher among the trees
lean against any one for solid help.
And her bones were turned to branches.

The trees break and you half fall
onto an overgrown and sunken avenue.
It curves along the contours and ends
where you end, in the gardens of the empty house.
Pass through the vacant rooms, the open windows,
you cannot lose yourself.

Dead, like they die in the theatre.
I imagine us here, on the sill of the big house
talking under the lintel of a doorway
you do not invite me through. Time strolls in the garden,
a heavy crop of pears that rots down each year,
the espaliered fruit trees, herbs, all grown wild.

I   EXT: The Mouth of Hell

A garden, as a child might draw it,
garden of bricks and blocky shrubbery:
by the fantastic urns and aristocratic hedges
two figures: he and she.
(Intertitle: '*How did you come here?*')
He wears a bedsheet toga and sandals,
plywood lyre propped on one arm.
This is the high pornography of 1907 –
she is naked, her hair undone.
('*Come with me, come back home.*')
The garden is poppies and thistles,
would be grey in Technicolor.
She wants to offer her hand,
as he reaches for it, she withdraws.
('*Do not look back. I will follow.*')
His white face strains at sorrow, turns away
back on the path he had taken.
What horrors have grown here?
The backcloth is painted shade and fingers.
('*I do not hear you. I must turn! I must!*')
And we do not see him turn.
Just a single shot of her in the garden.
A naked ghost, her dark eyes closed
and then, with a Méliès twist, she is gone.

II   INT: Her Flat

Two hundred seconds of ancient celluloid
threaded into the machine and thrown
in a square of light on their bedroom wall.
He winds the reel back, Eurydice
doomed always to try again.
She wears a willow-pattern dressing gown
and her high copper hair drawn up.

Her legs across his lap, and his hand
rests on them, at the top of the thigh.
The skin feels smooth – blue of the gown,
and the rain's blue light at the window.

III   M.O.S.

('*You can hear me, you can touch me.*')
Surreptitiously, other people cut themselves
into the film, and soon he is seeing them
as they shall be when they are the past.
Sweat sticks the hair to her forehead.
For one second he grasps her arm
and both recoil, for she has no skin
just a ghost of flesh on a smooth white bone.
I will not go through with this, she says
and she was not there any more.
An unattained wife. He passes on
through easily soluble mazes, old as core-ice,
calls hopelessly *Comrade* to those he sees.
('*I am not a shadow. I am not one of you.*')

9

I wrote to you last March in Madrid
to see if you were alive
Just give me time you could have said

you have broken yourself:
fragments are everywhere
a girl comes by with a different name

or a different passport
but with the same eyes
with the same mouth, with those small feet

Thick fog. I walked down the way of all flesh
and thought that I passed you, coming the other direction.
You looked like you were going home
or at least away from me with purpose
but you stopped   to hear your name.
Your shoulders showed you recognised my voice
even before you turned your painful eyes.
You tried to walk away   I held your wrist
What could I have done   to change
what happened? But you said   nothing
then freed yourself with distressing ease
and backed away again into the mist.

Your smile fades and the garden is now dark.
A world hides between your lips.
You kiss me so hard I feel your teeth
under my dry mouth captured by your mouth.

There is a sound of wings in the garden
in the distance a cuckoo, and autumn grows dark.
In the sky a moon far less white
than the small breasts I wrap in my arms.

My hands, which don't quite know what to do,
touch the fainting marble of your waist,
reach down to the place where all poems end,
the soft feathers around that lovely scar.

A breeze, and a fountain in the distance.
I touch my lips to the little wet sea snail of your ear.
When I get to the fence that surrounds this garden
I turn round to look for you one last time.

And once again my mouth feels the pressure
of those lips that I kissed without seeing them
while your hands played with my clothing:
my sombre black suit, my sad black tie.

after the Spanish of Pablo García Baena

Death is not the end; some doors are never fully closed,
and hollow ghosts escape their coffins and ovens.
She had been – she is – buried in rowdy Madrid,
but last night, as I held myself in a breaking sleep,
Carlota came to me and leant over my uneasy bed.
She was like her photographs, the same steady eyes;
her right ankle still had its tattoo. But her skin was broken,
and her clothes were rags covered with dirt and clay.
She was there, she could speak, I knew it was her,
but the thumb bones creaked in her fragile hands.
'How can you sleep,' she said, 'how can you sleep?
I knew this would happen, that you'd forget it all:
the windowsill where my arms wore two smooth dents,
the code to my staircase, the heavy metal doors.
We broke into a fire-watchers' tower and saw the city –
do you remember? – saw the city and made promises.
Were those light promises, are you allowed to forget?
Where were you when I died? Did you do anything?
If you had cried out for me to come back, I could have
at least for one day, I could have held myself alive,
but nobody, not you, not Julius, Arima, nobody…
None of you even knows where I am buried.
Would it cost you too much to find out, find me?
Is there anybody who talks about me with love,
who remembers me as I was, not just as someone
who died, who died young, who died too young?
You deserve to have me haunt you, keep you awake,
hurt you… but what's the use? You'll write your poems
which turn me into some amalgam of memory
and adolescent hard-on: I'm safe for you to use now.
Even these hands that grasp you, even these hands,
they'll just be one more image among the others.
At least I have been faithful, I haven't forgotten,
I remember you well and keep my mouth shut.
You can't negotiate with me: my arguments are fixed,
and I will keep my counsel.'
                                 She touched my shoulder
and I reached up to her, those remembered arms

and her torso cold and so thin. But she twisted away,
propped herself on her elbows and looked into my face.
'Find me. Do what you can for me, for my body.
Stop writing about me. I am not, I am not material
for you to appropriate and employ. Clean my grave,
lay some flowers there, give me an epitaph:
not one of your self-indulgent look-at-mes,
but something simple and worthy, for visitors
to read and understand. Of course, keep writing
but leave me out of it. And find other women
while you live: when you are dead you will be mine
alone, and we together shall be dust and ashes.'
She stopped talking, and lay down beside me,
but when I opened my eyes, my arms were empty.

after the Latin of Propertius

Coda

With two bags where his two hands were
he hieroglyphs through the barrier
into the underground kingdom
and waits for the train to come.

The sound of submerged bells
through the liftwells and sunken tunnels –
travelling lights shoal like fish over his face
as his coin-etched carriage pauses,

and he mounts long enough to recall when he had
in his arms one night that night's beloved
and felt the metro line pass close under her skin –
the whole structure shaking.

That girl across the track is just like her…
And then on metal stairs
through fathoms of doubt he forces and forces
his way, to the dim concrete surface.

Notes

p. 11

The poem which forms the basis for the first section of 'The Water Cycle' is Martín López-Vega's 'Fontana de Trevi' from *Elegías romanas* (2004).

p. 14

M.E. Hodges (1916-2009) was my maternal grandmother. A fact that, though strictly speaking irrelevant to 'Halfway Through the A-Feature', is nonetheless worth recording.

p. 18

The picture which was the immediate inspiration for 'Young Romance' is the cover for *Young Romance* magazine, Vol. 1 No. 150 (1967). For the time being, it can be seen online at http://trunt.blogspot.com/2008/03/pulp-1967-vintage.html.

p. 25

Some details in 'Tourism' come from oral testimony gathered and reported by Marfua Tokhtakhodzhaeva in her book *The Re-Islamisation of Society and the Position of Women in Post-Soviet Uzbekistan* (2008).

p. 29

'The Dogs of a House in Mourning and the Naked Girl' is based on an essay by the film director Nagisa Oshima, found in *Cinema, Censorship and the State* (1993).

p. 31

'Found Poem: President's Reminiscences Read Widely' was found on the Korean News Service website (http://www.kcna.co.jp/).

p. 34

Ivan Maisky (1884-1975) was a Soviet diplomat, ambassador of the Soviet Union to Finland, Japan and, between 1932 and 1943, to the UK. He was arrested in 1953 and sentenced to six years in prison, but was released in 1955 and later rehabilitated. While in prison, he composed a number of poems. I came across a list of the titles of some of them and adopted them for this sequence. The titles alone are Maisky's; having read a few of his actual poems, I can safely assert that they would not have been anything like mine.

p. 38

The epigraph to 'Likeness' comes from Katia Kapovich's 'In the

Bathhouse' from *Gogol in Rome* (2004).

p. 42
No reference is intended in 'The True Scholar' to any scholar – true or untrue, living or dead.

p. 45
A serviceable recipe for Dark and Stormys is rum, freshly squeezed lime juice and ginger beer in the ratio 1:1:3.

p. 51
The epigraph to 'Eurydice' is taken from Søren Kierkegaard. I found it in W.H. Auden's anthology *The Living Thoughts of Kierkegaard* (1952), which does not indicate where exactly the passage comes from.

p. 55
'Eurydice: 3'. Karl Blossfeldt (1865-1932) was a photographer, famous for his close-up studies of plants.

p. 57
'Eurydice: 5'. This is a free translation of Luis Rogelio Nogueras's 'Don't look back, lonesome boy' from *Las quince mil vidas de caminante* (1977).

p. 58
'Eurydice: 6'. The line 'es ist richtig so, Anna, aber so schwer' comes from the section 'Unzucht' (Lust) in Bertolt Brecht's *Die sieben Todsünden der Kleinbürger* (1933). 'It is right like this, Anna, but so hard.'

p. 61
'Eurydice: 8'. INT and EXT stand for Interior and Exterior. M.O.S. stands for Motor Only Sync, indicating that a scene is to be shot without any sound. The story that the term came into existence with the early influx to Hollywood of German directors not very fluent in English and is a corruption of 'mitout sound' is apocryphal.

p. 65
'Eurydice: 11'. This is a free translation of Pablo García Baena's poem 'Jardín' from *Rumor oculto* (1946).

pp. 66–7
'Eurydice: 12'. This is a free translation of Propertius IV, 7, 'Sunt aliquid Manes: letum non omnia finit'.